PHILOSOPHY ABOUT LIFE

PHILOSOPHY ABOUT LIFE

What is life? How to live?

Dr. François Adja Assemien

Copyright © 2021 by Dr. François Adja Assemien.

All rights reserved. No part of this book may be reproduced in any form or by any electronic or mechanical means, including information storage and retrieval systems, without permission in writing from the publisher, except by reviewers, who may quote brief passages in a review.

ISBN: 978-1-956736-10-6 (Paperback Edition)
ISBN: 978-1-956736-11-3 (Hardcover Edition)
ISBN: 978-1-956736-09-0 (E-book Edition)

Some characters and events in this book are fictitious. Any similarity to the real persons, living or dead, is coincidental and not intended by the author.

Book Ordering Information

Phone Number: 315 288-7939 ext. 1000 or 347-901-4920
Email: info@globalsummithouse.com
Global Summit House
www.globalsummithouse.com

Printed in the United State of America

FROM THE SAME AUTHOR

The African Rebels, novel, Page Turner, 2020
Introduction to philocure, essay, Edilivre, 2016
The Golden Rules of Personal Success, Happiness, Health and Salvation, Essay, Edilivre, 2016
Forbidden Africa, novel, Edilivre, 2016
The World is worth nothing, essay, Edilivre, 2016
Côte d'Ivoire hurts, essay, Edilivre, 2018
The Current slavery in Africa, essay, Global Summit House, 2020
The way to live in America, guide, Edilivre, 2019
Moral and spiritual education, manual, Edilivre, 2016
African Consciousness, essay, Edilivre, 2016
Electoral Code, novel, Black Stars, 1992
Portrait of the good and the bad voter, of the good and the bad candidate, essay, Black Stars, 2000
The Eleven Evils of Côte d'Ivoire, essay, Afro-Star, 2005
Côte d'Ivoire and its foreigners, essay, Black Stars, 2002
The African Guide to Philosophy, Humanities and Humanism, manual, 1985
Political Thought to Save Ivory Coast, essay, Afro-Star, 2003
Ahikaba, novel, Mary Bro Foundation Publishing, London, 2018
Thomas Sankara like Thomas More and Socrate, essay, Ouagadougou, 2020.
Let's save humanity and life, essay, Global Summit House, 2021
Corona virus, essay, Global Summit House, 2020

Contents

General Introduction viii
FIRST PART: LIFE IS FLEXIBILITY xi
  Introduction 1
  1. Intellectual Flexbility 3
  2. Moral Flexibility 7
  3. Physical Flexibility 10
  4. Flexibility In Politics 12
  5. Socio-Relational Flexibility 15
  6. Flexibility In Socio-Economic Life 18
  7. Flexibility in Artistic Crafts 20
  8. Flexibility in Science 23
SECOND PART: LIFE IS LOVE 27
  Introduction 29
  1. Life is a Factor of Union or Love 31
  2. Life is a Factor of Creativity 33
  3. Life is a Factor of Development 35
  4. Life is a Factor of Power 38
  5. Life is a Factor of Happiness 40
  Conclusion 43

General Introduction

Everyone talks about life. The vulgar man, the man in the street, the religious or theologian and the scientist or biologist talk about it. We, philosophers, also have our idea about life. Life is a fascinating subject which concerns and preoccupies all living men. It is said proverbially that if life is worth nothing, nothing is worth life. Everyone knows and recognizes that he is alive, that he lives well or lives badly. A proverb says that a living dog is better than a dead lion. Thus life is the object of universal critical judgment. We strive to value life, to appreciate it, to magnify it or, on the contrary, to denigrate and condemn it in the name of experiences and various trials we face. There are happy experiences and there are unhappy experiences. There are very painful trials and salutary trials. It is by all of this that we judge life. Because everything happens in life.

Life is the overall framework of our activities. It is the universal receptacle. All human actions take place in time and space. Life, time and space are inseparable. These three things are everything. They are consubstantial and correlative. They form a coherent whole or an organic unit. We cannot imagine life outside of time and space. And, conversely, we cannot imagine time or space without taking life into account. Life of each being is measured or expressed by duration (time) and takes place in space. Our identity includes our date of birth, our place of birth and our professional activity. These three things constitute life of the individual. Life is the sum of our presence in the world, of our identity and of our activity. This sum can please or displease, be glorious or condemnable. But my life is my life. It's my own property. Everyone likes to say that with arrogance. But, in reality, my life belongs to everyone since it is oriented, judged, controlled and governed or managed by others (looks, police officers, magistrates of the courts, moralizers, priests, pastors, Imams, gurus…). To identify and understand the concept of life, we must take all of this into account. It is to know that life is at the same time an individual and collective act(experience), an universal movement, that is to say the activity of the great Whole. Life is a fabric, a network of relationships or relationships that encompasses all beings and things located in time and space acting and interacting with each other.

All beings and all things are united, unified and confused in the great Whole, the universe, the cosmos. All are **brothers** .They are like drops of water in an ocean (cosmos). The common feeling that binds them all is **love** . Love is to be taken here in its broadest sense as what brings all beings together (men, animals, plants, air, water, gas, earth, minerals). Love is the link, the relationship of interdependence, of interaction between beings. It is the natural necessity for beings to be together, united, indissolubly linked. It is a natural, a cosmic law which governs the universe. Love is the fundamental or primordial law, the first cause, the causative cause not caused. All beings absolutely depend on law of love in order to be able to live, exist and be. Without love there is no life, there is no being. It is always the union or unity that produces being (the trinity: father, mother, child). Only the law of love allows all beings to live, exist and be. No being is isolated. The individual does not exist, cannot live or be. No being is separate from others and lonely. The solitary or individual being is a myth, a fiction. It is not a reality. The word individual is therefore meaningless. It is without content. Any being who opposes the law of love, like a rebel, resistant, disappears from this world. He suppresses himself. He's a suicidal man. Life is love. This is the supreme law of the world.

FIRST PART

LIFE IS FLEXIBILITY

INTRODUCTION

The essential attribute of human life is flexibility. Life is not something rigid, static, fixed, but rather a movement or a dynamic phenomenon. The living being is called to become flexible at any time and everywhere. Man must become more flexible in his intellectual, moral, physical, political, social, relational, economic, religious, aesthetic, scientific life. He is subject to this law of flexibility. Flexibility is the opposite of rigidity, stiffness, fixity, immobility, intolerance, dogmatism. Flexibility is synonymous with conciliation, reconciliation, understanding, harmony, balance, union, solidarity, cooperation, love, compassion, empathy, peace.

A flexible man is one who is not narrow-minded, closed, dogmatic, intolerant. It is the one who has the dialectical sense. He is open, permeable. He lets himself be transformed. He is modest, humble, realistic, objective, reasonable. He is understanding and sociable. He harmonizes with the world, with the values, norms and rules of society. So he is prudent, wise. He has no enemy. The wise man is loved and accepted by all. Everyone likes him. He does not offend anyone, does not frustrate anyone, does not seek to dominate others. He respects the opinions, ideas, beliefs, principles, truths, falsehoods, prejudices, lies and delusions of people. So he is at peace with others. He avoids creating conflicts, palaver, harmful polemics. He puts everyone at ease. He is polite, disciplined, wise. He avoids violence that is engendered and nourished by hatred, vanity, pride, narcissism, self-centeredness, intolerance, dogmatism, resentment, anger, frustration and desire for domination .

The flexible man accepts everyone. He knows that no one is perfect on earth. So he is forgiving, kind, benevolent. In the chapters that follow, we will show precisely and concretely what intellectual, moral, physical, political, social, relational, economic, aesthetic, scientific flexibility consists of.

1

INTELLECTUAL FLEXBILITY

We are talking here about the attitude of the thinking and speaking subject towards others. Anyone who expresses ideas and communicates with others must observe certain rules of good conduct. As speaker and interlocutor, he must know how to listen and understand others without showing pride, vanity, contempt for others (his interlocutors). Despite his very high level of culture, education, erudition, a speaker must display politeness, courtesy, humility and respect for others. In conversations, he should not insult, scoff, frustrate others, call them ignorant, idiots, fools. He must not ridicule them, make fun of them. He must not allow himself to systematically refute their opinions, their ideas, their knowledge. He should not force them to give up. If he talks to them and nags their beak, he puts himself in danger. He will not be listened to, respected or accepted. Even if he produces ideas and knowledge in gold and diamonds, he will not be listened to or respected. His knowledge will be useless, vain, sterile. People will refuse it. He will be hated and persecuted. And he will have deserved it. It's his fault. He lacked tact, circumspection, pedagogy, common sense, good manners, **flexibility**. The whole thing is not the knowledge which one possesses but the way with which one behaves towards others. When you are hated by others, you are no longer useful to them. You are no longer worth anything in their eyes, even with all your gold and all your diamonds.

Let us know that conversation is a place of exchange and sharing. In this context, no one should, a priori, believe himself to be superior to others. No one should take himself for a god to be worshiped. Even in the classroom, a teacher should be humble and modest towards his students. He should be polite, non-arrogant, not insolent, not haughty. He must avoid being too smug, contemptuous and insulting. Otherwise he will be vomited, hated by his students. Good conduct or good character is everything. It is worth its weight in gold in all interpersonal, social and educational situations and relationships. No one likes or accepts contempt and violence towards him. No one accepts the intellectual domination and authoritarianism of others over him, no matter where they comes from. Contempt, violence and domination of the master, the boss and the knowing or scholar are fought by all. "You can only command nature by obeying it," said Francis Bacon. Likewise, men are only commanded by obeying them. This serious flaw or lack of wisdom cost the lives of Jesus Christ and his disciples. Nietzsche underlines this well by saying that Jesus was not careful. On this level, Asian thinkers, philosophers and scholars are superior and exemplary. They are not dictators, dominators and imperialists. They do not offend anyone or any people. They are true sages or saints. Indeed, we can only and really bring light to men if we are polite, respectful, disciplined, humble, virtuous. Otherwise we are a hateful poison. Socrates understood this so well that he took care to tell his interlocutors (the sophists) that he only knew his ignorance. "All I know is I don't know anything," he said humbly.

Moreover, knowledge is relative and subjective. What does it mean to be intellectually flexible? This means that we must avoid putting too much value on our knowledge to the detriment of the knowledge of others. There is sensible knowledge and scientific knowledge. Sensitive knowledge, testimonies of our five senses, is of less value than scientific knowledge which is rationally and technically established in the laboratory of physics, chemistry, biology. Scientific knowledge is experimental. It stems from the observation of natural phenomena, from technical experimentation in the laboratory, from hypotheses drawn from observation, and then results in the law. This law is the truth sought and discovered. It is applied everywhere and remains constant, general. It reflects the cause-and-effect relationship that exists between two successive phenomena in time and space, the first of which is the cause and the second the effect. It is the most accurate and certain knowledge. It is verified by its multiple applications in the daily life of humans. It is efficient, practical. It makes it possible to manufacture and invent various and useful machines and tools. "Science hence law, law hence forecast, forecast hence action", said Auguste Comte. All humans have sensitive, vulgar, immediate or intuitive knowledge. It is uncertain, doubtful, subjective, unreliable. It is based on sensation and perception. At this level, every one has his truth. I see the world as I am and not as it is in itself and for itself (subjectivity and relativity). As for scientific knowledge, it belongs exclusively to privileged specialists called scientists (physicists, chemists, biologists). There are also the so-called human, social or moral sciences: sociology, anthropology, history, linguistics, economics, law, psychology, ethnology. They imitate the method of the exact sciences, physics and chemistry. However, they cannot achieve the certainty and effectiveness of the latter. They lack rigor. Science is deterministic or it is not. Unlike the physico-chemical sciences which provide quantitative laws (explanatory, measurable), the human or social sciences provide qualitative laws (descriptive).

The knowing or the scholar is an agent of knowledge. He has scientific culture. His knowledge is correct. It is not a simple opinion, a prejudice, a religious dogma, a rumor ("we say"), a fiction or a myth. To be true, thought must use the scientific, dialectical approach, that is to say borrow the ternary method which examines everything in depth by confronting several theses (thesis, antithesis, synthesis). Truth emerges from discussion, analysis and synthesis of ideas. To really think is to reflect, that is to say to doubt, to criticize, to decompose, to recompose, to deconstruct and to reconstruct ideas. **Such is intellectual flexibility**. Truth, as a quality of thought, is the fruit of flexibility, of acrobatics of intelligence or of the mind. A narrow-minded, rigid, dogmatic mind can find neither the truth nor the solution of a problem. Truth is both formal (identity or coherence between ideas) and material (conformity to reality). Truth is a construction of Reason (Logical Reason and Dialectical Reason). Scientific or natural law is a discovery resulting from the confrontation of Reason with experience (knowing subject facing the world or object to be known).

2

Moral Flexibility

In the realm of action or personal conduct, man needs flexibility. He must respect both his personal morals and the morals of others. Morality organizes the life of humans in society, in nature and in the universe. It governs order. It establishes laws or rules that we must follow in order to live well, to be happy, in peace, insecurity and in good health. Laws or moral rules aim to protect and maintain order, balance and harmony within the individual, society and the world. It's called **discipline** . Each person must be disciplined. He must submit to the laws and rules coming from society, Reason, the universe and nature. We must be chameleons,that is to say flexible(adapt) and not rigid,refractory, unruly. Likewise, each people or each society must be a chameleon, that is to say conform to its own laws or rules and to the laws and rules of the world (nature and universe). Otherwise it will be chaos and unhappiness for all.

Each of us has found order (discipline, institutions, norms, customs) in society and in the world. He must obey it. Obedience to the law (order) is freedom, justice, security, peace, harmony, balance, happiness, salvation. Disobedience to the law is disorder, anarchy, doggy, imbroglio, savagery, barbarism, violence,injustice, danger, death. The violation of prohibitions (offenses, crimes) is catastrophic for all. Obedience to one's own moral rules is wise, virtuous. Obedience to the moral rules of one's society (customs) is a duty. This is payable, required. Obedience to foreign rules or customs is also a duty. This is payable. And this is the hardest, the most difficult. This is the big problem with race, interethnic, intertribal, international and intercontinental relations. We are made to live together, with others. The proof is that we travel. We leave our world and we go to others. Humans enter into mixed marriages. Thus we are obliged to practice and respect the laws, habits and customs of others. We are forced to adapt and conform to cultures or values around the world. This reflects flexibility. There are, of course, differences and conflicts between the cultures of the different peoples of earth. But this must be overcome and smoothed out with flexibility, wisdom and necessary sacrifices. It is possible and common. Mixed marriages would not exist without this fact. This is how the African peoples can cooperate, collaborate with all the other peoples of earth (Americans, Europeans, Asians, Oceanians).

In your relationship with yourself, things are very simple. You can obey your own rules and habits or change them at any time. It all depends on your will, your Reason, your conscience, your desire and your current needs or interests. You change inexorably with time and circumstances. You are flexible. You are not fixed, irremovable. You transform yourself whenever it is useful or necessary. Being is not. The non-being is. We are all non-being, becoming, change, movement, chameleon (suppleness, flexibility). At the social and collective level, it is compulsory, exigible. We must adapt and submit to the order, to the discipline in force under penalty of being excommunicated, ostracized, rejected, fought (police, prison). The outcasts, the critics and the marginalized people are condemned, persecuted or killed (Socrates, Thomas More, Karl Marx, Jesus Christ, Seneca, Cicero, Martin Luther King Junior, Malcolm x...).

Family, professional, religious, moral and civic education models us, shapes us, socializes us and makes us flexible (loyalty, patriotism). We are integrated into order and collective discipline. It is flexibility.

3

PHYSICAL FLEXIBILITY

Our physical body is the perfect expression of flexibility. See how our four limbs are harmoniously articulated. There are joints all over our body. This is done to make us flexible. Our body is elastic. The muscles are flexible. This is how a woman's vagina expands to allow the baby to come out of her mother's womb. Flexibility is a natural law. It is fundamental. It is universal. It is essential for the life of all beings. Molluscs, reptiles, felines, plants, air and gas owe their existence and their salvation to flexibility. How could a snake move, run, fight, struggle for food if it lacked flexibility? Since it has no feet or arms on which it could lean to start, leap, launch and move forward. How could it climb trees without feet and arms? How could it kill his prey (a large animal) and swallow it if it was not flexible, elastic, agile? Its small mouth expands until it lets a large doe, a crocodile or a human being pass through its constantly expanding belly. The snake owes everything to its extreme flexibility. It is a bungee cord. It uses its body which is a strong elastic cord to tie up, strangle, suffocate and kill its prey. This is the inestimable value of physical flexibility as a natural phenomenon.

In humans, physical flexibility also plays a very large role in daily life. Indeed, it allows us to move, to do all our gestures and to accomplish all our tasks. Men are more or less physically flexible. Some are naturally very flexible while others cultivate flexibility through sports, work and various physical exercises. All humans have an interest in cultivating the agility of the body as much as possible because it allows for a good and healthy life. With that, we are very comfortable in the practice of martial arts (judo, karate, kung fu…). Indeed, in this area, you have to be like a snake or a cat. You have to be the wind. This makes it easy to win fights. This is the basic virtue for combatants. Flexibility gives efficiency. You have to work on your body, educate it, shape it through various relaxation exercises. This is taught in dojos, clubs (Fitness), videos. It is necessary to supplement the natural, organic, muscular flexibility by the artificial acquired flexibility. It slows down old age and the process of dying.

This work on his body gives good health. It strengthens the immune system, gives a vital tone. So we have longevity. Man can live on earth for a very long time. He can live for centuries (200 or 300 years) as yogis and Taoists show us by leading a very disciplined and very pure life morally, mentally, spiritually,socially and physically (sadhus, yogis, Taoists). Healthy, powerful organic life (health, wellness) is founded on the cultivation of flexibility. Human longevity is the result of work on his body. It is the result of sport(yoga).Let us kill the ignorance, the illusion or the lie that one can live a long healthy life and experience well-being without intense physical activity or sport. Let's drive away our laziness and neglect. Let's be rubber. Let's be water. Let's be air or wind. It is very beneficial for us.

4

FLEXIBILITY IN POLITICS

What is flexibility in politics? How to practice it? What are its positive results or benefits? What are the disadvantages of the deficit of flexibility in politics? Every citizen of a country is in politics. And he is facing politics. He is a political agent and subject. He is called upon to vote on laws, to participate in the choice of the societal model, the regime or the political system, the leaders or rulers. His opinion and his voice count in the making of national decisions in a democratic and republican system. What should be his general attitude towards his political obligations?

He must accept collective decisions and respect them unreservedly and without reticence. He must respect the established order and the democratically adopted regime. The voice of the people is the voice of God, the saying goes. The voice of the people is sacred. "Obedience to the law that we have prescribed is freedom," said Jean-Jacques Rousseau. It makes everyone happy and safe. Anarchy or dread is not profitable to anyone. No individual is at peace or happy in the disorder, barbarism, savagery and chaos reigning in his country. This fact imposes on him the duty to be disciplined, reasonable, wise, civilized, compliant. He must accept the principle of living together. He must practice the values, habits Philosophy

About Life and customs of his society. He's got to harmonize with that and come to terms with that. He must fit into the order and be loyal.

The virtues of a good citizen are obedience to laws, submission to the societal order (moral code, legal code, religious code etc.), that is to say loyalty, civility, patriotic devotion. This constitutes citizen flexibility.

The advantages of civic flexibility lie in the fact that everyone finds himself in social peace, security and happiness. The balance and the political stability of a country promote his progress and prosperity. If not, everyone sinks into the abyss. The rebellious, iconoclastic, marginal citizens (outcasts) are ostracized, banished, put to death (Socrates, Thomas More, Jesus Christ). Popular consensus or the expression of the general will must be respected by all citizens. Let us be flexible and democratic. As well in the republic as in the monarchy. In any state. Let's respect all the political rules. Let us avoid injustice, arbitrariness, savage, barbaric violence. Living together is synonymous with flexibility. Flexibility is synonymous with consensus, solidarity, union, discipline, loyalty, righteousness, patriotism, good citizenship, cooperation. In short, politics is softness, respect for all by all. All citizens are equal in rights and dignity. They are equal before the law. Law and liberty are a general agreement.

We are in a system which requires the total alienation of each associate with all his natural rights to the whole community. Each giving himself entirely, the condition is equal for all. And the condition being equal for all, no one has an interest in making it onerous for others. The alienation being done without reserve, the union is perfect and no partner has anything more to claim. As each gives himself to all, finally he gives himself to no one other than himself, in the name of reciprocity. There is balance, fairness, harmony and justice in equality of condition. The strength of each becomes the strength of all, that is to say the strength of the community. Thus we obtain the City and the Republic (body politic, State, Sovereign, Power). This is how the peoples are formed. The associates call themselves citizens as participants in the sovereign authority and subjects as subject to the laws of the state. The social pact means that whoever refuses to obey the general will will be forced to do so by the whole body: he will be forced to be free. What man loses by the social contract is his natural freedom and an unlimited right to whatever tempts him and which he can attain. What he gains is civil liberty and ownership of everything he owns (Jean-Jacques Rousseau, in **Du Contrat Social**).

5

SOCIO-RELATIONAL FLEXIBILITY

It is a question here of giving rules of interpersonal skills and of knowing how to live with people. We are in community. Our life always takes place in community. We meet people everywhere, in family, in town, in village, in our neighborhood, in our country, in our place of work, of leisure, in travel, abroad etc. We communicate at all times with our fellow human beings, verbally,by phone, by internet, in writing (books, letters, newspapers), by radio, television, videos ... We forge multiple bonds of friendship, fraternity , collegiality, collaboration, bilateral and multilateral cooperation and conjugal or matrimonial ties. We want to talk here about the quality of these links. All our links with others must be based on politeness, courtesy, friendship, love, compassion,empathy, solidarity, mutual aid, trust. Because these values represent the foundation and the pledge of well-being,peace,security, understanding, good understanding, harmony, success, happiness, good health.

These values exclude violence, arbitrariness, injustice, contempt, insolence, arrogance, disdain, insult, affront, rudeness, indiscipline, hostility, animosity, hatred, intolerance, dogmatism, the spirit of revenge, authoritarianism, dictatorship, resentment, selfishness, egocentricity. The properly human, interpersonal, intercommunity relationships are horizontal and not vertical. Indeed, they exclude domination, oppression, exploitation, nuisance and require as main virtues moral integrity, honesty, humility, the spirit of justice, equity, equality, of brotherhood.

We are not here in the relationship of executioner to victim, of master to slave. All who are involved in this type of relationship are free, equal in rights and in dignity. They are siblings to each other as they are all humans and not animals, plants and minerals. So everyone must respect everyone. Everyone must love everyone. This promotes the maintenance of the community, strengthens family, friendship, inter individual, professional ties. This imposes on everyone the duty to be flexible in their existence and in their life. Being flexible means being able to adapt to everyone and being able to adapt to societal and community life in all its details. It is submitting to the requirements of the group, to the needs of one's community. It is respecting moral, legal, social and religious rules. It is to obey the habits and customs in force in one's environment. It is to integrate perfectly, harmoniously with the order which reigns. It is to humanize oneself by accepting the discipline of the group to which one belongs and wherever one finds oneself. It is the condition which allows the individual to live and be happy in this world. It is about being like a grain of sand, like a drop in an ocean, like a snake, like a chameleon, like a monkey. All of these beings are characterized by the same qualities. They are flexible, agile and adapted to their environment. They harmonize with their surroundings. It is difficult to separate, to distinguish a grain of sand from the other grains together forming earth or the sand. Likewise, it is difficult to separate or distinguish the drops from the ocean. Because every drop taken is the whole ocean. It contains all the chemical components of the ocean. The chameleon, meanwhile, takes the color of the environment where it is located. It transforms and adapts to its environment. It merges with its environment and even becomes sometimes invisible. As for the snake, it is like rubber. It is very flexible. It rolls up and becomes a ball. This allows it to avoid dangers. It goes everywhere without difficulty, without risk. It falls to the ground, climbs trees, shrinks, stretches out, runs without feet, zigzags. It swallows its prey while swelling. It kills them using its body as an elastic rope that allows him to tie them up, suffocate them, strangle them. It expands. The monkey jumps from tree to tree. Its wings in air. It is a very good acrobat. It rolls on the ground and in the air. These are useful and very salutary cases of flexibility. So we have to cultivate flexibility in life, physically, mentally, socially.

You have to know how to choose your relationships and know how to leave them, when it is necessary, with flexibility, elegance, diplomacy, wisdom in order to avoid any danger. You should not say loud and clear everything you think of someone in his presence. Not all truth is good to say. We must avoid shocking, hurting, frustrating others. We must avoid judging and condemning sharply, without reserve, without holding back others. The truth creates enemies. It is sometimes a danger for friendship.

6

Flexibility In Socio-Economic Life

Happiness of the individual depends on his skill and wisdom. An individual who is flexible in mind and in body is bound to be happy. He is successful in this world. On the contrary, an individual who is not flexible in mind or in body is necessarily unhappy. He fails everywhere. He cannot make a success of his life in the world. Skill, flexibility and wisdom are synonymous here. It is a duty, an imperative, for each person to have intelligence and strength to create the human, material, financial, economic resources that are necessary to meet his personal and family needs. Likewise, a government must have all the necessary capacities to produce the goods and wealth that are necessary for the life and happiness of its people. The general condition of life and happiness of man and of society is called work. It is the creative effort or the capacity to produce the goods and the riches of life. This ensures comfort, well-being, freedom, security, independence, dignity, prosperity for each and everyone. The unemployed and the idle people are not happy, free, dignified, secure. Work is any physical, manual or intellectual activity which results in the creation of goods and the means of life. It is a utilitarian act and not a hobby. It is not free or disinterested because it provides us with money (salary)

which allows us to meet our needs (food, housing, clothing, health, education of children).

All work is useful and honorable. There is no such thing as a foolish profession, but foolish people. It is unemployment and idleness that are dishonorable and degrading. It makes man miserable, poor, vicious, dishonest, unworthy and contemptible. Voltaire said, rightly, that "Work takes away from us three great evils: boredom, need and vice". So giving everyone a job is like closing prisons. Anyone who refuses to work is a fool. He is dangerous because he will end up harming others. He will be, for example, thief, robber, burglar, crook. He is unfair and harmful to order. The one who sorts and hates jobs and dreams too much instead of doing the job that is available to him is an idiot. Indeed, he prefers to be unemployed or to be idle. He voluntarily makes himself needy and indigent. He will be a beggar or a thief. "Yours is better than two you get," the saying goes. He thinks wrong and lives in illusion. He lacks wisdom, flexibility. In life, you have to know how to go step by step in business, in all things. You should not refuse a chance that is offered to you today (however small it maybe). You have to seize every little job opportunity that presents itself to you. It doesn't matter how good that work is. You have to do it while waiting to have the job of your dream. It doesn't take you away from your dignity. Quite the contrary. Humility precedes glory. It pays a lot. You can start your professional life at the bottom of the social ladder and progress gradually to the top, until you become a boss. So nursing aides became nurses and then doctors. Teachers became college professors and then university professors. This is the result of socio-economic flexibility. If you have this flexibility, you can become a great man or at least earn a decent living. It requires patience, modesty, humility, simplicity and excludes foolish pride, vanity. So we can embellish our life from day to day, gain victories, gain ranks.

7

FLEXIBILITY IN ARTISTIC CRAFTS

In artistic professions, we produce the beautiful, the pleasant. The artist must be able to please everyone. He must be able to satisfy all tastes. He should not be limited to producing the pleasure of the eyes (colors, gestures) or of the ears (sounds) for himself or for a very small number of people if he seeks full success. Everyone wants fun, happiness, cheerfulness, joy. To be an artist is to work for all humans or to serve humanity. The artist is a seller of pleasure, of happiness. As such, he must expand his market and his clientele. Take the case of musicians all over the world. They are facing all of humanity. They are listened to everywhere and by everyone. So, they have to know the different tastes and the different cultures of the world. The inhabitants of earth follow artistic, musical fashions. They are snobs. But they are locked into their cultures and artistic traditions. If the Ivorian artist, for example, wants to fully succeed in his career, it will be in his interest to go to all countries and imitate their musical cultures. He will have to do everything to make them accept his product or his merchandise. It will have to play everyone's music and please people of all countries. It will have to satisfy the taste of all audiences. His music will have to resemble the chameleon, that is to say take all the musical colors of the world.

Rhythms and musical sounds vary from society to society. They are not universal. But the artist must be universal, popular, chameleon. He should not be content to practice the only rhythm and the only sonority of his locality. His audience and global fanatics expect more from him. Everyone wants to benefit from his art and his talent. If we take the case of an Ivorian artist, he must take into account the needs and tastes of 60 ethnic groups living in Côte d'Ivoire. 60 ethnic groups mean 60 different cultures and 60 different rhythms or musical styles.

Each ethnic group has its own rhythm or musical style. Thus the Bété do not dance and sing in the same way as the Senoufo, Abouré, Baoulé, Akyé, Ebrié, Mbatto etc. The Ivorian musician, wanting to be national, has a duty to make all these peoples dance and to amuse them by the rhythm of his music. Further, he must be able to play to cheer up and delight the Congolese, Ghanaians, Malians, Guineans, Burkinabè, Senegalese, Togolese, Beninese, Cameroonians, French, Germans, Italians, English, Chinese, Americans ... Such is the vision and the philosophy of what Dr. Kamamo calls **Abubu music** (our music). Abubu music is the musical synthesis of all genres and all musical styles. It is universal music. All the inhabitants of earth recognize themselves in the Abubu music. They appreciate it and love it. It is their common music. They say everywhere: "Well done, Dr. Kamamo!". It is a fine example of musical chameleonism. It is an important symbol of artistic flexibility. It is an exemplarity or a model to imitate. Songs like "The Woman", "Liberation Fight", "African, Free Yourself", "African Merits", "Stop Corona Virus", belong to all world musical cultures. The form and substance of these pieces touch all oppressed peoples who love peace, justice, liberty, well-being, equality, security, dignity, happiness and salvation. The author of these pieces sensitizes all the oppressed and pushes them to claim the values which are their legitimate rights. The Abubu music rhythm is universal.

The themes sung in this music are also universal (love, beauty, freedom, justice, humanism, happiness, peace, health, security, unity, fraternity, equality, independence, sovereignty, human rights etc.).

8

Flexibility in Science

Science is a process, an approach, a method which gives us the highest form of knowledge. It is the most certain knowledge, the most effective because it is tested, experienced or applied in our daily life. Its application is called technique or technology which has now become indispensable to humanity. Science requires flexibility which is expressed in vigilance, discipline, honesty and intellectual rigor. One does not discover a scientific law or the truth by gratuitous, fanciful, dogmatic statements. Science is opposed to opinion, dogma, lies, prejudice, rumor, illusion, belief, supposition and all that pertains to metaphysics, religion, superstition. These are thoughts not verified, demonstrated, unproven, not reasoned, not criticized in the laboratory (intuitive, immediate, revealed, vulgar knowledge). Science requires critical thinking, in-depth, methodical, analytical, synthetic thinking. It requires the verification, the demonstration, the experimentation of any judgment, any speech or affirmation. It relies on coherent, i.e. logical, mathematical reasoning that demonstrates ideas on the basis of material, objective and abstract evidence. It requires extreme caution, honesty and humility. "You can only command nature by obeying it," said Francis Bacon. Auguste Comte said:

"Science hence law, law hence forecast, forecast hence action". Without these three things there is no science. This is the most perfect definition of science. Indeed, science is deterministic or not. The scientific process successively includes the observation of a phenomenon, the formulation of a hypothesis as a future law, the technical experimentation of this hypothesis in the laboratory as verification and, finally, the formulation of the law or truth.

This is the way in which the scientist (physicist, chemist, biologist…)constructs or discovers the truth. He starts from a fact (or effect that he has observed) and goes back to its cause. He links the phenomenon to its cause. It is then said that he explained the phenomenon. He made it known, that is to say, he unveiled a cause and effect link or a causal relation which wants to be constant, necessary and generalizable. This is how one arrives at the feeling of certainty in science. Scientific work therefore proves that flexibility is essential for thought to be true and useful or effective. The subject-knowing who finds himself in front of an object to be known must be flexible. He must be patient and disciplined. He must not lie to himself or deceive the world. The truth is his passion. This must make him honest, persevering, objective. He must not take a rumor, a prejudice, a religious dogma, a myth, a vulgar, fanciful opinion for truths. He absolutely must submit these things to rigorous, uncompromising criticism. It consists of checking everything, examining everything minutely through reasoning, demonstration and technical experimentation. This is scientific objectivity which is opposed to lies, illusion, prejudice, religious dogma, mystery. There is no place for miracles, for magic. Nothing is obtained here by prayer, by dreaming. Science is a rational, conscious and dynamic activity of the mind, of the intelligence. It is a confrontation of mind with reality to draw certain, irrefutable knowledge. Science is controversy. Where there is no controversy, debate, criticism, calculation of ideas,verification to be done, there is no science. There is simply religion which imposes dogmas and so-called sacred things that the faithful or believing sheep must adore. Faith is stupid. It is madness. It is a disease of soul. It forbids knowledge, critical thinking, doubt, skepticism, rationality. It prevents men from knowing the truth about the world. It says, for example:"happy are those who believe without doubting, without having seen". Religion says that only the fools, the dunces, the morons, the naive, the gullible and the superstitious will be saved. The religious spirit is turned towards magic, illusion, superstition, fanaticism, followingism (relation of the shepherd to the sheep).

The religious spirit is lying, dogmatic, rigid, obscurantist, narrow-minded, irrational. It refuses discussion, reasoning and doubt which free men from ignorance, fear, demystify things. Thus religion kills the mind and Reason (superior and salutary faculties of man). It animalizes us. It makes sheep, slaves, submissives, the mentally insane. Every religious is mentally ill. Religion is a drug. It is the opium of the people according to Karl Marx. It prevents people (the flock of sheep) from seeing, understanding, knowing reality, defending themselves, being happy and saved. It is the most formidable weapon of the oppressors, predators and imperialists. It makes mankind blind, stupid and infantilizes us. Thus religion promotes evil, allows oppression, domination and exploitation of man by man (the class struggle). It is an imperialist, colonialist and slave ideology. It is categorically opposed to science which enlightens, humanizes, calms and frees man from fear (based on the superstition of god, of the invisible world, of hell, of the beyond ...) of the unknown, of ignorance, of domination and of exploitation. Science heals and saves man.

SECOND PART

LIFE IS LOVE

Introduction

We are life. We live life. We are in life. Life is in us. Everything is life. Life is everywhere. All of these expressions and many more can be heard. They come out of the speeches of theologians, philosophers, scientists, psychologists and vulgar men. Everyone thinks he knows the origin, nature and value of life. Everyone tries to write, explain and interpret life. We all try to give meaning, value to life or to our life. It strengthens us and keeps us alive. We say: "Even if life is worth nothing, nothing is worth life". Some hate, despise, insult and quit life while others praise it, glorify it, bless it, cling to it and savor it. Who is wrong and who is right? Everyone is wrong and everyone is right. Everyone has a personal and different life experience (or reading). So our judgments about life are relative and subjective. We do not all have the same attitude to life. We do not all have the same outlook on life. We are different from each other. Men's behavior and judgments about life depend on their situation, condition, status and personality. The slave or the prisoner has his own way of judging and considering life. His life disgusts him and makes him embittered. He condemns it and curses it. This is not the case with his master. The slave master or the bourgeois does not hate ,curse or condemn life he leads. The poor and the rich do not judge life in the same way. Some poor and needy kill themselves. They would rather die than suffer, live on,vegetate,toil, pull the devil by the tail everyday. For them, it is not all about living. On the other hand, some say: "A living dog is better than a dead lion". Our conceptions and visions of life are all subjective. Everyone has his morals, his mentality and his ideology or philosophy about life.

Men are not unanimous on the issue of life. Here we want to elucidate the concepts of life and love. We want to show their nature, their functions and the dialectic that binds them. Life is a whole. It is the whole which includes our actions, our thoughts, our feelings as a global, complex phenomenon, taking place in time and in space. Individual or collective life is a succession of things, facts, situations, actions, events. It starts from birth to death. It is biological, sociological, psychological. The living human thinks, acts and experiences feelings, emotions, passions. He lives with people, in society. He weaves diverse, complex and infinite links with others. Man always lives with others, by others and for others. Any action that man takes, any act he takes, any feeling he experiences and all his thoughts are aimed at and concern others. It absolutely tends towards others.

Man is in a permanent relationship with the world because he lives in the world. The world is made up of everything. It includes humans, animals, plants, water, gas, air, earth, minerals, energy, fire, matter… The world is a web of coherent relationships. All beings are interdependent in this network. They are related to each other. The world is on the move. It is dynamic and not frozen or static. It is constantly evolving, transforming, developing, recreating, degrading and rebuilding itself. Man is included in this world movement which is called history. Man is the product of history. And he himself is the agent or motor of history, of its history. Life is movement or history. Man is the creator of life and life is the creator of man.

1

LIFE IS A FACTOR OF UNION OR LOVE

Life is a movement and a receptacle. This movement or dynamism shapes and maintains man in his destiny of union, community, society, group. Life as receptacle is the shelter or habitat of beings. It brings together the beings it has created. Living together, beings develop actions, thoughts, feelings etc. They get to know each other. They rub shoulders, communicate with each other. They influence each other by sharing time and space between them. They are linked by several social contracts(marriage, procreation, family, citizenship, work, solidarity, cooperation etc.). Marriage unites men and women. It creates the family community. It unites parents and their children. It also unites families between them (exogamy), countries between them,continents between them, tribes, clans, ethnic groups and races between them (biologico-cultural interbreeding).

To live is necessarily to be with others, to unite with others, to form a family, a village, a town, a country, a nation, a tribe, a clan, a caste. To live is to cooperate or collaborate with others in the context of work and all activities that require association with others, participation in organizations, in the life of a group, of a team (profession, sport, religion, army, party or popular revelry, politics). Life is spent in groups and associations. It is a collective and a community act. Man has nothing and is nothing without his relationships with others who create him, educate him, maintain him, protect him, defend him, enrich him, keep him alive, save him and make him happy . It is a question of sharing the culture of a people with others and of carrying all the cultural symbols of this people (name, identity, language…). The being of every human is therefore collective.

We are all members of a family, a society, a culture, an ethnic group, a group. Life is a huge invisible chain. Each thing or being constitutes a visible link in this chain. Life is a whole and each of us is a part of it. Ultimately, life is unity. It is a rigorously structured or organized system. The different elements in this system are inseparable. So the family is alive. It is in the system we call life. It multiplies, branches out. The ancestors produced the grandparents who. The grandparents in turn begot the parents. The latter produced the children who in turn will produce children and so on. It is a long chain of uninterrupted solidarity. Several associated families who live in the same space form a village. This village grows to become a city. Several cities living in the same space create a country. Several countries of the same continent can unite and form a federation (the United States of America, Russia, Switzerland, Nigeria…). Society is an organic, coherent, homogeneous whole. Its culture is a system or structured set of values, institutions, rules, regulatory norms (morality, positive law, religion, politics, economy, art, technology, philosophy, cosmogony, worldview, ideology, myths, eschatology , science, knowledge, paradigms). These are the characteristics of life as a dynamic whole, a system of functions.

2

LIFE IS A FACTOR OF CREATIVITY

Life leads people to create, to produce, to invent things. How? Life creates needs in us and forces us to struggle to create things to satisfy them or to disappear. Life is dynamism, creative activity. It is progress, evolution. It is history and development in every way. We are life from which we think, act, create and procreate. Humans, animals and plants are multiplying and spreading all over the world. It is a natural, universal phenomenon. Living is expression of cosmic, natural energy. It is not passive, inert, sterile. It is prolific, procreative, inventive. So man works. By working, he expresses himself, asserts himself, strengthens, develops, builds himself, improves, perfects himself. He transforms his condition and his primary being, natural, animal, into virtues, into values or into social, moral, intellectual qualities. Thus he developed science, technology, religion, philosophy, institutions, art, law, morals, politics.

Man feels the need to constantly create tools, machines and instruments that are useful for his existence in the world. He is faced with difficulties and challenges that he must overcome in order to preserve himself. He does not want to disappear like certain beings who disappear for lack of imagination, intelligence and creative and salutary capacity. Thus he knows how to adapt to his natural and social environment. There are his strength, his greatness, his power and his superiority to other beings. Man is then the measure of everything according to Protagoras. Blaise Pascal said that man is a thinking reed. He thus underlines his capacity to surpass and overcome his weakness, his fragility and his physical smallness thanks to the intelligence and the Reason which he possesses. René Descartes affirms that "Science and technology will make men as masters and owners of nature". Indeed, Reason allows man to compensate and transcend his faults and his natural helplessness. So man is like the king of universe. He explores it, exploits it and dominates it. He appears very dangerous and formidable to other beings. Civilization is against nature. The acquired dominates the innate. Universe created man and man modifies universe, transforms it according to his needs and his taste. Man remakes, reconstructs the world thanks to his Reason, his intelligence and his creative imagination. He changes the world. He develops the world and his life quantitatively and qualitatively thanks to his industrial, technical, scientific, philosophical activity. Man imposes his will on the world, directs and partly controls it, subjectively. Man is a thinking subject facing the world which is an object to think about, to know, to use.

3

LIFE IS A FACTOR OF DEVELOPMENT

Life forces us to develop ourselves and to develop our world. What do these expressions mean: to develop, to develop the world and development? The general idea that appears under these notions is the idea of extension, elevation, improvement, amendment, correction, improvement, enlargement, enrichment, power. It is about putting ourselves in value, putting things and our world in value in order to make the most profit of life. This consists in creating the ideal conditions for our life or in equipping ourselves with adequate, effective, powerful means which promote our life, our development and our well-being. This is how life, a biological phenomenon, leads us to **existence,** as a philosophical, moral concept. In other words, life forces us to think, create, evolve, progress and be happy.

Development is our action or our daily struggle to achieve certain ends, an ideal, better world. It is our noble, legitimate fight to get out of our precarious, purely animal condition, our savage, primitive state and to achieve a civilized, human, dignified and salutary state. It is the search for security, perfect health, convenience, ease, happiness, prosperity, wealth (existence). This is both quantitative and qualitative development. Life is given to us by nature. Existence is our product, our work. This work is never finished, perfect. It is a permanent fight which is called development, that is to say progress, work or all the conscious, considered and voluntary activities of man. It is unique to man. The human being has desires and needs which he must satisfy or else disappear. To live, man must eat (food), sleep (housing), move (road, vehicle), take care of himself (medicine), dress (clothing), get married (sexual pleasure, family), have fun, play (leisure). The human being organizes his existence by creating values, institutions which guarantee him security, health, happiness, salvation (family, civil society, community, laws, police, army, morals, religion, positive law, government, state).

Its quantitative and qualitative development consists in the realization of works of general interest, that is to say in the creation of social, health, school, road, security infrastructures (housing, jobs, hospitals, schools, police, army, church, administration, government). It is a question of establishing a policy in the world which regulates the economic, social and political questions to promote happiness and salvation of all. The promotion and defense of ethical, moral, religious or spiritual values are essential, fundamental and primordial. This is vital and guarantees order, security, justice, cohesion, harmony and balance within civil society. This makes it possible to avoid barbarism, violence, vices, disorder, evil, instability, the decadence of society. A society without morality and without rights is unlivable. It is a jungle in which the strongest kills and devours the weak with impunity. The strong have the right to life and death over the weak. They take all the goods and all the wealth of the country. Everything is on their own. They are the masters and the others are their slaves. The only right which reigns there is the right of the strongest. Only the master is free, in peace, in security and happy. Man is then forced to develop the virtues of ascetic morality which save him from all dangers and evil. This is the reason to be of qualitative development. Man needs justice, freedom, equality, fraternity, love, peace, security, that is to say intangible, abstract values which complement and balance his objective, quantitative or measurable development (industrialization of his environment). It is about technical, economic, social, political, cultural, civilizational, scientific development.

4

LIFE IS A FACTOR OF POWER

Man is power. Society is power. Nature is power. Universe is power. Everything is power or force. Human beings organize, develop, cultivate and rationally use their power. This is how they rule the world. The power of the individual is reflected in his capacity to act, to think, to work, to produce, to create things. His body is equipped with defensive agents that fortify him and prevent him from falling ill or succumbing to external aggressions. He possesses Reason, intelligence, conscience and will which are major assets ensuring him success and triumph over the world. So he is inventive. Everything he does makes him powerful: work, sport, art, technique, science, religion, philosophy, thought, feeling. He has material, physical, mental, moral, psychological power.

Man produces his life, transforms himself and creates history. His power is infinite. It is the power of cosmos, of nature. He is the great All, the alpha and the omega. Everything is in him and he is in everything. "Man is a thinking reed," says Blaise Pascal. This means that he is at the same time weak, fragile and powerful. This is the human paradox. The man who walks, runs, speaks, gestures, moves, exercises power. When he eats, laughs, sings and dances, he exercises power. When he makes love, he exercises creative or procreative power. When he gives commandments to others and dominates, he exercises power. When he also obeys orders, he exercises power, but over himself. By submitting to constraints, he dominates himself and exercises his inner, moral and psychological power. He frees himself as a civilized citizen, disciplined vis-à-vis the laws of his society. He frees himself thanks to his reasonable will. "Obedience to law that we have prescribed is freedom," says J.-J. Rousseau (**Du Contrat social**). Thus man exercises his inner power. The polite child who obeys his parents' orders exercises his inner or moral power. By integrating into the societal order, he exercises power. It consists in overcoming, in dominating one's natural, purely animal impulses and instincts. He learns to be a man, worthy and responsible. He fulfills his family and civic duties. In doing so, he obtains rights over others. He therefore exercises his inner power, family power and societal power.

He becomes the owner and manager of collective values as an accomplished man or citizen. He is then a perfect moral agent and legal agent. So he can become a leader, a king, a President, an authority. He exercises public power, supreme power, political power. He makes decisions (decrees, laws, ordinances) that apply to society, nature, universe and all orders: human order, animal order, plant order and things (water, air, gas , mineral..).

5

LIFE IS A FACTOR OF HAPPINESS

Life is movement. It is dynamism, activity, change of state, of nature, of value. It is filled with events, situations, circumstances. It contains everything, what we like and what we dislike, what we prefer and what we hate, what we adore and what we hate etc. We fight to create or preserve things that give us joy, pleasure and happiness. We are bathed in happiness. Happiness is everywhere. It filled our life. So we don't see that we are happy. We hear people say here and there that they are looking for happiness, that they are not happy. It is neither paradoxical nor absurd. Indeed, when we are melted (or confused) in a thing, we do not see it. When we become one with something, we do not see it. It is the principle of fusion, of confusion, of osmosis, of the removal of distance, of separation. We are united with happiness, we cannot see it. To be able to see something, you have to move away from it. You have to keep a distance from it. There is no misfortune. Or else misfortune is too rare. It is so rare that the day it comes in the form of momentary pain, annoyance, and suffering, we will exaggerate it and take it to cover and obscure the ocean of happiness that we live in all the time. What is rare is valuable. Whether it's something positive or negative.

It is very unfair and abnormal. We must understand that happiness is paramount in our life. It is the essence of life. Happiness is an ocean and misfortune is a small piece of waste which floats on the surface of a wave which will be quickly rejected, deposited on the shore. Misfortune is filth that the ocean does not like. The ocean rejects all the dirt. We must therefore learn to despise misfortune as an epiphenomenon, that is to say something temporary, ephemeral, without consistency or value. Let us put misfortune in its rightful place and above all make sure that it does not prevent us from living fully nor from savoring the happiness which is eternal and infinite. All living are happy. Only the dead are not. Life is happiness. Such is its intrinsic value.

Conclusion

Life is conceived here as a coherent, inclusive whole, a dynamism, a synthetic global movement. We have shown that everything depends on everything, that everything is in everything, that the world is made of everything, that all things and all beings are complementary, united, interdependent, and form an organic unit, very well structured. This dialectic should not be seen at the level of human beings alone, or of the relationships between them, of the relationships between their various activities, creations, institutions, practices. We must go further. It is also necessary to see the natural world, outside, the universe. It is necessary to seethe harmony, the balance, the complementarity between all the phenomena and all the realities of the world (love). We must think about the dialectical relationships between humans, animals, plants, minerals, water, gas, air, fire, energy (the reciprocal action of each thing on other things and of each being on other beings). The infinite multiplicity of things and beings in the world acting on (or against) others is flexibility. The notion of flexibility is understood here in a very broad sense. Flexibility here means exactly dialectic, duality, interaction, mutual, reciprocal influence, harmony, balance. In short, everything is in everything, everything is with everything, everything is against everything or union, exclusion, love, hatred, complementarity. All of this is flexibility as a movement or global, natural, universal activity. Flexibility dominates all relationships, all activities in each individual, in society, on earth and in the universe. Flexibility is presented here as the spring or engine of history and of the world. It is the centerpiece of society and individual life. It is about life in all its compartments and in all its dimensions: intellectual life, moral life, social life, political life, physical life, bodily life, economic life, aesthetic life, artistic life, scientific life… Flexibility is the general rule or standard, the essential basis, the central pillar of existence. It is innate and acquired, that is to say that it is cultivated and developed at the personal, human and societal level (diplomatic relationship between States). It is natural elsewhere, in other beings and things. Flexibility is the main mistress of the world, the matrix of the universe, of nature, of society and of the individual. It merges with love-hate. This is the fundamental message of this book.

Book Summary

Philosophy about life is a way of living. It is the art of living with wisdom. It is a light. It is a very valuable tool made available to everyone. Its goal is to help people correct their life, improve themselves, create the conditions for their happiness, their success and their salvation.

www.ingramcontent.com/pod-product-compliance
Lightning Source LLC
LaVergne TN
LVHW040201080526
838202LV00042B/3273